Book 1

Python Programming In A Day

BY SAM KEY

&

Book 2

Ruby Programming Professional Made Easy

BY SAM KEY

Book 1

Python Programming In A Day

BY SAM KEY

Beginners Power Guide To Learning Python Programming From Scratch

Programming Box Set #35: Python Programming in a Day & Ruby Programming Professional Made Easy

Table Of Contents

Introduction

I want to thank you and congratulate you for purchasing the book, "Python Programming in a Day: Beginners Power Guide To Learning Python Programming From Scratch".

This book contains proven steps and strategies on how you can program using Python in a day or less. It will contain basic information about the programming language. And let you familiarize with programming overall.

Python is one of the easiest and most versatile programming languages today. Also, it is a powerful programming language that is being used by expert developers on their complex computer programs. And its biggest edges against other programming languages are its elegant but simple syntax and readiness for rapid application development.

With python, you can create standalone programs with complex functionalities. In addition, you can combine it or use it as an extension language for programs that were created using other programming languages.

Anyway, this eBook will provide you with easy and understandable tutorial about python. It will only cover the basics of the programming language. On the other hand, the book is a good introduction to some basic concept of programming. It will be not too technical, and it is focused on teaching those who have little knowledge about the craft of developing programs.

By the way, take note that this tutorial will use python 3.4.2. Also, most of the things mentioned here are done in a computer running on Microsoft Windows.

Thanks again for purchasing this book. I hope you enjoy it!

Chapter 1: Getting Prepared

In developing python scripts or programs, you will need a text editor. It is recommended that you use Notepad++. It is a free and open source text editor that you can easily download and install from the internet. For you to have the latest version, go to this link: http://notepad-plus-plus.org/download/v6.6.9.html.

Once you install Notepad++ and you are ready to write python code lines, make sure that you take advantage of its syntax-highlighting feature. To do that, click on Language > P > Python. All python functions will be automatically highlighted when you set the Language to python. It will also highlight strings, numbers, etc. Also, if you save the file for the first time, the save dialog box will automatically set the file to have an extension of .py.

To be able to run your scripts, download and install python into your computer. The latest version, as of this writing, is 3.4.2. You can get python from this link: https://www.python.org/download.

And to be able to test run your python scripts in Notepad++, go to Run > Run... or press the F5 key. A small dialogue box will appear, and it will require you to provide the path for the compiler or a program that will execute your script. In this case, you will need to direct Notepad++ to the python executable located in the installation folder.

By default or if you did not change the installation path of python, it can be found on the root folder on the drive where your operating system is installed. If your operating system is on drive C of your computer, the python executable can be found on C:\Python34\python.exe. Paste that line on the dialogue box and add the following line: $(FULL_CURRENT_PATH). Separate the location of the python.exe and the line with a space, and enclosed the latter in double quotes. It should look like this:

```
C:\Python34\python.exe "$(FULL_CURRENT_PATH)"
```

Save this setting by pressing the Save button in the dialogue box. Another window will popup. It will ask you to name the setting and assign a shortcut key to it. Just name it python34 and set the shortcut key to F9. Press the OK button and close the dialogue box. With that setting, you can test run your program by just pressing the F9 key.

By the way, if the location you have set is wrong, the python executable will not run. So to make sure you got it right, go to python folder. And since you are already there, copy python.exe, and paste its shortcut on your desktop. You will need to access it later.

And you are all set. You can proceed on learning python now.

Chapter 2: Interactive Mode – Mathematical Operations

Before you develop multiple lines of code for a program, it will be best for you to start playing around with Python's interactive mode first. The interactive mode allows a developer to see immediate results of what he will code in his program. For new python users, it can help them familiarize themselves on python's basic functions, commands, and syntax.

To access the interactive mode, just open python.exe. If you followed the instructions in the previous chapter, its shortcut should be already on your desktop. Just open it and the python console will appear.

Once you open the python executable, a command console like window will appear. It will greet you with a short message that will tell you the version of python that you are using and some command that can provide you with various information about python. At the bottom of the message, you will the primary prompt (>>>). Beside that is the blinking cursor. In there, you can just type the functions or commands you want to use or execute. For starters, type credits and press Enter.

Mathematical Operations in Interactive Mode

You can actually use the interactive mode as a calculator. Try typing 1 + 1 and press Enter. Immediately after you press the Enter, the console provided you with the answer to the equation 1 + 1. And then it created a new line and the primary prompt is back.

In python, there are eight basic mathematical operations that you can execute. And they are:

- Addition = 1 + 1
- Subtraction = 1 – 1
- Multiplication = 1 * 1

- Division = 1 / 1

In older versions of Python, if you divide integers and the division will result to a decimal, Python will only return an integer. For example, if you divide 3 by 2, you will get 1 as an answer. And if you divide 20 by 39, you will get a zero. Also, take note that the result is not rounded off. Python will just truncate all numbers after the decimal point.

In case you want to get an accurate quotient with decimals, you must convert the integers into floating numbers. To do that, you can simply add a decimal point after the numbers.

- Floor Division = 1 // 1

If you are dividing floating numbers and you just want to get the integer quotient or you do not want the decimals to be included, you can perform floor division instead. For example, floor dividing 5.1515 by 2.0 will give you a 2 as an integer quotient.

- Modulo = 1 % 1

The modulo operator will allow you to get the remainder from a division from two numbers. For example, typing 5 % 2 will give you a result of 1 since 5 divided by two is 2 remainder 1.

- Negation = -1

Adding a hyphen before a number will make it a negative number. You can perform double, triple, or multiple negations with this operator. For example, typing -23 will result into -23. Typing --23 will result into 23. Typing -----23 will result into -23.

- Absolute Value = abs(1)

When this is used to a number, the number will be converted to its absolute value or will be always positive. For example, abs (-41) will return 41.

Python calculates equation using the PEMDAS order, the order of operations that are taught in Basic Math, Geometry, and Algebra subjects in schools. By the way, PEMDAS stands for Parentheses, Exponents, Multiplication, Division, Addition, and Subtraction.

Chapter 3: Interactive Mode – Variables

During your Math subject when you were in grade or high school, your teacher might have taught you about variables. In Math, variables are letters that serve as containers for numbers of known and unknown value. In Python or any programming language, variables are important. They act as storage of values. And their presence makes the lives of developers easy.

However, unlike in school, variables in programming languages are flexible when it comes to their names and functions. In Python, variables can have names instead of a single letter. Also, they can also contain or represent text or strings.

Assigning Values to Variables

Assigning a value to a variable is easy in Python. You can just type the name of your variable, place an equal sign afterwards, and place the value you want to be contained or stored in the variable. For example:

```
>>> x = 151
```

When you assign a value in a variable, Python will not reply any message. Instead, it will just put your cursor on the next primary prompt. In the example, you have assigned the value 151 to the variable x. To check if it worked, type x on the console and press Enter. Python will respond with the value of the variable x.

Just like numbers, you can perform arithmetical operations with variable. For example, try typing x – 100 in the console and press Enter. Python will calculate the equation, and return the number 51 since 151 – 100 = 51. And of course, you can perform mathematical operations with multiple variables in one line.

By the way, in case that you did not define or assign a value to a new variable, Python will return an error if you use it. For example, if you try to subtract x with y, you will get an error that will say name 'y' is not defined. You received that message since you have not assigned anything to the variable y yet.

In addition, you can assign and change the value of a variable anytime. Also, the variable's value will not change if you do not assign anything to it. The variable and its value will stay in your program as long as you do not destroy it, delete it, or close the program.

To delete a variable, type del then the name of the variable. For example:

```
>>> del x
```

Once you try to access the variable again by typing its name and pressing Enter after you delete it, Python will return an error message saying that the variable is not defined.

Also, you can assign calculated values to a variable. For example:

```
>>> z = 1 + 4
```

If you type that, type z, and press Enter, Python will reply with 5. Variables are that easy to manipulate in Python.

You can also assign the value of one variable to another. Below is an example:

```
>>> y = 2

>>> z  = y
```

The variable z's value will be changed to 2.

Chapter 4: Interactive Mode – Strings

Your program will not be all about numbers. Of course, you would want to add some text into it. In Python, you can do that by using strings. A string or string literal is a series of alphanumeric numbers or characters. A string can be a word or sentence. A lone character can be also considered as a string. To make your program display a string, you will need to use the print function. Below is an example on how to use it:

```
>>> print ( "Dogs are cute." )
```

To display a string using the print function properly, you will need to enclose the string with parentheses and double quotations. Without the parentheses, you will receive a syntax error. Without the quotes, Python will think that you are trying to make it display a variable's value.

By the way, in older versions of Python, you can use print without the parentheses. However, in version 3 and newer, print was changed to as a function. Because of that, it will require parentheses.

For example:

```
>>> print ( "Dogs" )
```

That line will make Python print the word or string Dogs. On the other hand:

```
>>> print ( Dogs )
```

That line will return a variable not defined error. With that being said, you can actually print or display the content of a variable. For example:

```
>>> x = 14
>>> print ( x )
```

The print function will display the number 14 on the screen. By the way, you can also use single quotes or even triple single or double quotes. However, it is recommendable to use a single double for those who are just started in program development.

Assigning Strings to Variables

Assigning strings to variables is easy. And it is the same as assigning numbers to them. The only difference is that you will need to enclose the string value in double quotations or reverse commas as some developers call them. For example:

```
>>> stringvariable = “This is a string.”
```

If you type stringvariable in the interactive mode console, it will display the This is a string text. On the other hand, if you do this:

```
>>> print ( stringvariable )
```

Python will print the string, too.

Strings can include punctuation and symbols. However, there are some symbols or punctuations that can mess up your assignment and give you a syntax error. For example:

```
>>> samplestring = “And he said, “Hi.””
```

In this case, you will get a syntax error because the appearance of another double quote has appeared before the double quote that should be enclosing the string. Unfortunately, Python cannot recognize what you are trying to do here. Because of that, you need the by escaping the string literal.

To escape, you must place the escape character backslash (\) before the character that might produce conflict. In the example's case, the characters that might produce a syntax error are the two double quotes inside. Below is the fixed version of the previous paragraph:

```
>>> samplestring = “And he said, \”Hi.\””
```

Writing the string assignment like that will not produce an error. In case you print or type and enter the variable samplestring in the console, you will see the string that you want to appear, which is And he said, “Hi.”.

Escape Sequences in Python

Not all characters are needed to be escaped. Due to that, the characters that you can escape or the number of escape sequences are limited. Also, escape sequences are not only for preventing syntax errors. They are also used to add special characters such as new line and carriage return to your strings. Below is a list of the escape sequences you can use in Python:

- \\ = Backslash (\)
- \" = Double quote (")

- \' = Single quote (')
- \b = Backspace
- \a = ASCII Bell
- \n = Linefeed
- \f = Formfeed
- \t = Horizontal Tab
- \r = Carriage Return
- \v = ASCII Vertical Tab

Preventing Escape Sequences to Work

There will be times that the string that you want to print or use might accidentally contain an escape sequence. Though, it is a bit rare since the backslash character is seldom used in everyday text. Nevertheless, it is still best that you know how to prevent it. Below is an example of an escape sequence that might produce undesirable results to your program:

```
>>> print ( "C:\Windows\notepad.exe" )
```

When Python processes that, you might encounter a problem when you use since the \n in the middle of the string will break the string. For you to visualize it better, below is the result:

```
>>> print ( "C:\Windows\notepad.exe" )
C:\Windows
otepad.exe
>>> _
```

To prevent that you must convert your string to a raw string. You can do that by placing the letter r before the string that you will print. Below is an example:

```
>>> print ( r"C:\Windows\notepad.exe" )

C:\Windows\notepad.exe

>>> _
```

Basic String Operations

In Python, you can perform operations on your strings. These basic string operations also use the common arithmetical operators, but when those operators are used on strings, they will produce different results. There are two of these. And they use the + and * operators. Below are examples on how to use them:

```
>>> print ( "cat" + "dog" )

catdog

>>> print ( "cat" * 3 )

catcatcat

>>> _
```

When the + operator is used between two strings, it will combine them. On the other hand, if the multiplication operator is used, the string will be repeated depending on the number indicated.

By the way, you cannot use operators between strings and numbers – with the exception of the multiplication symbol. For example:

```
>>> variable_x = 1 + "text"
```

The example above will return an unsupported operand type since Python does not know what to do when you add a string and a number.

Chapter 5: Transition from Interactive Mode to Programming Mode

Alright, by this time, you must already have a good feel on Python's interactive mode. You also know the basic concepts of variables, strings, and numbers. Now, it is time to put them together and create a simple program.

You can now close Python's window and open Notepad++. A new file should be currently opened once you open that program. The next step is to set the Language setting into Python. And save the file. Any name will do as long that you make sure that your file's extension is set to .py or Python file. In case the save function does not work, type anything on the text file. After you save it, remove the text you typed.

Now, you will start getting used to programming mode. Programming mode is where program development start. Unlike interactive mode, programming mode requires you to code first, save your file, and run it on Python. To get a feel of the programming mode, copy this sample below:

```
print ( “Hello World!” )

print ( “This is a simple program that aims to display text.” )

print ( “That is all.” )

input ( "Press Enter Key to End this Program" )
```

If you followed the instructions on the Getting Prepared chapter, press the F9 key. Once you do, Python will run and execute your script. It will be read line by line by Python just like in Interactive mode. The only difference is that the primary prompt is not there, and you cannot input any command while it is running.

Input Function

On the other hand, the example code uses the input function. The input function's purpose is to retrieve any text that the user will type in the program and wait for the Enter key to be pressed before going to the next line of code below it. And when the user presses the key the program will close since there are no remaining lines of code to execute.

By the way, if you remove the input function from the example, the program will just print the messages in it and close itself. And since Python will process those lines within split seconds, you will be unable to see if it work. So, in the following examples and lessons, the input function will be used to temporarily pause your scripts or prevent your program to close prematurely.

You can use the input function to assign values to variables. Check this example out:

```
print ( "Can you tell me your name?" )

name = input("Please type your name: ")

print ( "Your name is " + name + ".")

print ( "That is all." )

input ( "Press Enter Key to End this Program. \n" )
```

In this example, the variable name was assigned a value that will come from user input through the input function. When you run it, the program will pause on the Please type your name part and wait for user input. The user can place almost anything on it. And when he presses enter, Python will capture the text, and store it to variable name.

Once the name is established, the print function will confirm it and mention the content of the name variable.

Data Type Conversion

You can also use the input function to get numbers. However, to make sure the program will understand that its numbers that it will receive, make sure that your input does not include non-numeric characters. Below is a sample code of an adding program:

```
print ( "This program will add two numbers you would input." )

first_number = input ( "Type the first number: " )

second_number = input ( "Type the second number: " )

sum = int(first_number) + int(second_number)

print ( "The sum is " + str(sum) )

input ( "Press Enter Key to End this Program. \n" )
```

In this example, the program tries to get numbers from the user. And get the sum of those two numbers. However, there is a problem. The input function only produces string data. That means that even if you type in a number, the input will still assign a string version of that number to the variable.

And since they are both strings, you cannot add them as numbers. And if you do add them, it will result into a joined string. For example, if the first number was 1 and the second number was 2, the sum that will appear will be 12, which is mathematically wrong.

In order to fix that, you will need to convert the strings into its numeric form. In this example, they will be converted to integers. With the help of the int function, that can be easily done. Any variable will be converted to integer when placed inside the int function.

So, to get the integer sum of the first_number and second_number, both of them were converted into integers. By the way, converting only one of them will result into an error. With that done, the sum of the two numbers will be correctly produced, which 3.

Now the second roadblock is the print function. In the last print function, the example used an addition operator to join the The sum is text and the variable sum. However, since the variable sum is an integer, the operation will return an error. Just like before, you should convert the variable in order for the operation to work. In this case, the sum variable was converted to a string using the str function.

There are other data types in Python – just like with other programming languages. This part will not cover the technicalities of those data types and about the memory allocation given to them, but this part is to just familiarize you with it. Nevertheless, below is a list of a few of the data type conversion functions you might use while programming in Python:

- Long() – converts data to a long integer
- Hex() – converts integers to hexadecimal
- Float() – converts data to floating-point
- Unichr() – converts integers to Unicode
- Chr() – converts integers to characters
- Oct() – converts integers to octal

Chapter 6: Programming Mode – Conditional Statements

Just displaying text and getting text from user are not enough for you to make a decent program out of Python. You need your program to be capable of interacting with your user and be capable of producing results according to their inputs.

Because of that, you will need to use conditional statements. Conditional statements allow your program to execute code blocks according to the conditions you set. For you to get more familiar with conditional statements, check the example below:

```
print ( "Welcome to Guess the Number Game! " )

magic_number = input ( "Type your guess: " )

if ( magic_number == "1" ):

   print ( "You Win!" )

else:

   print ( "You Lose!" )

input ( "Press enter to exit this program " )
```

In this example, the if or conditional statement is used. The syntax of this function differs a bit from the other functions discussed earlier. In this one, you will need to set a conditional argument on its parentheses. The condition is that if the variable magic_number is equal to 1, then the code block under it will run. The colon after the condition indicates that it will have a code block beneath it.

When you go insert a code block under a statement, you will need to indent them. The code block under the if statement is print ("You Win!"). Because of that, it is and should be indented. If the condition is satisfied, which will happen if the user entered 1, then the code block under if will run. If the condition was not satisfied, it will be ignored, and Python will parse on the next line with the same indent level as if.

That next line will be the else statement. If and else go hand in hand. The have identical function. If their conditions are satisfied, then the program will run the code block underneath them. However, unlike if, else has a preset condition. Its condition is that whenever the previous conditional statement is not satisfied, then it will run its code block. And that also means that if the previous conditional statement's condition was satisfied, it will not run.

Due to that, if the user guesses the right magic number, then the code block of if will run and the else statement's code block will be ignored. If the user was unable to guess the right magic number, if's code block will be ignored and else's code block will run.

Conclusion

Thank you again for purchasing this book!

I hope this book was able to help you to understand the basic concepts of programming and become familiar in Python in just one day.

The next step is to research and learn looping in Python. Loops are control structures that can allow your program to repeat various code blocks. They are very similar to conditional statements. The only difference is that, their primary function is to repeat all the lines of codes placed inside their codeblocks. Also, whenever the parser of Python reaches the end of its code block, it will go back to the loop statement and see if the condition is still satisfied. In case that it is, it will loop again. In case that it does not, it will skip its code block and move to the next line with the same indent level.

In programming, loops are essential, Truth be told, loops compose most functionalities of complex programs. Also, when it comes to coding efficiency, loops makes program shorter and faster to develop. Using loops in your programs will reduce the size of your codes. And it will reduce the amount of time you need to write all the codes you need to achieve the function you desire in your program.

If you do not use loops in your programs, you will need to repeat typing or pasting lines of codes that might span to hundreds of instances – whereas if you use loops in your programs, those hundred instances can be reduced into five or seven lines of codes.

There are multiple methods on how you can create a loop in your program. Each loop method or function has their unique purposes. Trying to imitate another loop method with one loop method can be painstaking.

On the other hand, once you are done with loops, you will need to upgrade your current basic knowledge about Python. Research about all the other operators that were not mentioned in this book, the other data types and their quirks and functions, simple statements, compound statements, and top-level components.

To be honest, Python is huge. You have just seen a small part of it. And once you delve deeper on its other capabilities and the possible things you could create with it, you will surely get addicted to programming.

Finally, if you enjoyed this book, please take the time to share your thoughts and post a review on Amazon. We do our best to reach out to readers and provide the best value we can. Your positive review will help us achieve that. It'd be greatly appreciated!

Thank you and good luck!

Book 2
Ruby Programming Professional Made Easy

By Sam Key

Expert Ruby Programming Language Success in a Day for any Computer User

Programming Box Set #35: Python Programming in a Day & Ruby Programming Professional Made Easy

Programming Box Set #35: Python Programming in a Day & Ruby Programming Professional Made Easy

Table Of Contents

Introduction

I want to thank you and congratulate you for purchasing the book, *"Professional Ruby Programming Made Easy: Expert Ruby Programming Language Success in a Day for Any Computer User!"*

This book contains proven steps and strategies on how to write basic lines of code in Ruby. This is especially made for amateur programmers with little to no experience in coding.

Ruby is a programming language which people think is ideal for newbies in the programming field. Congratulations on choosing this programming language. In this book, you will be introduced to all the fundamental aspects of coding in Ruby.

This book will give you a huge boost in your programming skills. However, it is also important to quickly supplement yourself with advanced Ruby tutorials after you are done with this book to retain the knowledge you gain from it.

Thanks again for purchasing this book, I hope you enjoy it!

Chapter 1: Setting Up

This book will assume that you are a bit familiar with computer programming and have made a few lines of codes in some languages. Also, from time to time, the book will provide further explanation of terms and methods that can easily confuse new programmers. In case you encounter a foreign term in the discussion, just take note of it since it and other such terms will be discussed later.

Before anything else, get the latest stable version of Ruby from the web. As of this writing, Ruby's stable version is 2.1.5.

Go to https://www.ruby-lang.org/en/documentation/installation/. In there, you can get the right installer package for the operating system that your computer is running on.

Be mindful of what you are going to download. Many people tend to download the source code of Ruby instead of the installation packages.

Take note of the location or directory where you will install Ruby. Once you are done with the installation, open Ruby's interactive shell.

For people who are using a computer running on Windows, you will find the interactive interpreter inside the bin folder located inside your Ruby installation folder. The file is named irb.bat. If you have installed Ruby using the default location, the interactive shell will be located at: "c:\Ruby21\bin\irb.bat".

What is the interactive shell anyway? In Ruby, you can program using two modes: the interactive mode and the programming mode.

Ruby's Interactive Mode

The interactive mode is an environment wherein Ruby will provide immediate feedback in every line of code or statement you type in to it. It is an ideal environment where new Ruby programmers can test and experiment with codes quickly. You will be using this mode in most parts of this book.

The interactive mode or shell will appear like a typical console or command prompt. In the shell, you should be familiar with two things. First is the cursor. Second is the prompt.

The cursor indicates where you can type or if you can type anything. In the interpreter shell, you can use overtype mode on this by pressing the insert key on your keyboard. You can return to insert mode by pressing the insert key again.

The prompt will look like this: irb(main):001:0>. If this prompt is on, it means that Ruby is ready to accept a line of code or statement from you. For now, type a letter a in the prompt and press the Enter key. The shell or interpreter will move the cursor, show a bunch of text, and display the prompt once again:

```
irb(main):001:0> a
NameError: undefined local variable or method 'a' for main:Object
        from (irb):1
        from C:/Ruby21/bin/irb:11:in '<main>'
irb(main):002:0>
```

This time, type "a" on the shell and then press the Enter key. Instead of an error, you have received => "a". Now, type "1" without the quotes. Just like before, the interpreter just provided you with a reply containing the number you entered.

Why does the letter a without the quotes returned an error? As you can see, Ruby provided you with an error message when you just entered the letter a without quotes. In Ruby, characters enclosed in double or single quotes are treated differently.

In the case of the letter a, Ruby understood that when you input "a" with the quotes, you meant that you are inputting the letter a. On the other hand, Ruby thought of something else when you input the letter a without the quotes, which will be discussed later.

You will receive error messages like the one before or other variations of it if you input something that violates Ruby's syntax or something that is impossible to be evaluated or executed by the interpreter. In simple terms, Ruby will provide you notifications like that if it does not understand what you said or cannot do what you commanded.

Now, type "1 + 1", without the double quotes, and press the Enter key. Instead of an error, you will receive this instead:

```
=> 2
```

Every time you press the Enter key, the shell check the command or statement you created. If it does not violate the syntax, it will proceed on checking if every word and symbols you placed make sense. Once the statement passes that check, it will evaluate and execute the statement and provide a result or feedback.

In this case, Ruby has evaluated the addition operation you commanded and replied the number 2, which is the sum of 1 + 1. Just before the number 2, an equal sign and "greater than" sign were placed. Those two denotes that the next value is the result of the statement you entered.

You might have thought that Ruby can be a good calculator. Indeed it is, but statements like "1 + 1" and "a" are only processed like that in the interactive mode of Ruby. If you include a line like that when coding in programming mode, you will certainly encounter a syntax error.

Ruby's Programming Mode

On the other hand, the programming mode is a method wherein you can execute blocks of code in one go. You will need to type the code of your program first before you can run and see what it will do.

You will need a text editor to type your program. Any simple text editor such as Notepad in Windows is sufficient for programming Ruby. However, to reduce typos and keyword mistakes, it is advisable that you use a source code editor, which will provide you with syntax highlighting and checking. In Windows users, a few of the best source code editors you can use for Ruby programming are Notepad++, TextWrangler, JEdit, and Crimson Editor.

Once you are done typing your code, save it as a .rb file. For Windows users: if you have let Ruby associate .rb and .rbw files to it, all .rb files or Ruby code you have created can be opened by just double clicking on them. They will act as if they are typical Windows program.

By the way, programming mode does not provide instant reply to your expressions. For example, if you input a = 1 + 1 in interactive mode, it will reply with => 2. In programming mode, that statement will not provide any output.

Also, if one of the lines encounters an error, the program will stop executing the next lines after the line that generated the error.

Chapter 2: Ruby Syntax

In the first chapter, you have encountered your first syntax error. For those who are not familiar with the term syntax, syntax is a set of 'language' rules that you must follow in order for a programming language (in this case, Ruby) to understand you.

A programming language's syntax is similar to English grammar where you need to correctly arrange parts of the sentence—such as verbs, nouns, and adjectives—to make it coherent and grammatically correct.

The two major differences between Ruby's syntax (or other programming languages' syntax as well) and English's set of grammar rules are Ruby's syntax's strictness and inflexibility. It is set to behave like that because computers, unlike humans, cannot understand or comprehend context. Also, if computers understand context and programming languages' syntaxes become lax, computer programming will become difficult.

First, computer will become prone to misunderstanding or misinterpreting your statements. If you point to a jar of jam in a shelf full of jars and requested people to get the one you want, most of them will surely get and give you the wrong jar. That kind of situation will happen if a programming language's syntax became loose.

Here are some of Ruby's syntax rules:

Whitespace

Whitespace (continuous spaces and tabs) are ignored in Ruby code unless they are placed inside strings. For example, the expression "1 + 1", "1   + 1", or 1+1 will provide the same result in Ruby.

Line Ending Terminators

New lines and semicolons are treated as line endings. Ruby works by reading your program's lines one by one. Each line is considered a statement. A statement is a combination of keywords, operators, values, methods, and properties, which is translated as a command.

Every time you put a semicolon or move to the next line, the previous line will be treated as a statement. There are some cases that if you do not place a semicolon but used a new line character (the one that the Enter key produces and pushes the cursor to move to the next line) to write a new line of code will make Ruby think that the previous line and the new line of code is just one statement. For example:

```
irb(main):001:0> 1 +
irb(main):002:0* 1 +
irb(main):003:0*
```

If you typed that in Ruby's interactive mode, you will not encounter an error or reply from Ruby. Instead, it allowed you to move on to the next line and type another line of code.

If you have noticed, the greater than sign at the end of the prompt changed into an asterisk. The asterisk denotes that all the succeeding lines of code after the previous one will be treated as one statement in Ruby or the next lines are meant to be continuations of the previous line.

Ruby behaved like that since you left an operator at the end of the line and did not place a value on the operator's right hand side. So, Ruby is treating the example as 1 + 1 +. If you place another 1 at the last line, Ruby will interpret that 1 as the last value to your expression and evaluate it. It will then produce a reply, which is => 3.

Case Sensitivity

Identifiers or names of constants, variables, and methods in Ruby are case sensitive. For example, a variable named Variable1 is different from variable1.

Comments

In computer languages, comments are used to serve as markers, reminders, or explanations within the program. Comments are ignored by Ruby and are not executed like regular statements.

Some convert statements in order to disable them. It is handy during debugging or testing alternate statements to get what they want since deleting a statement may make them forget it after a few minutes of coding another line.

To create comments in Ruby, use the hash sign (#) to let Ruby know that the succeeding characters is a comment line. You can insert comments at the end of statements. For example:

```
irb(main):001:0> #This is a comment.
irb(main):002:0* 1 + 1
=> 2
irb(main):003:0> 1 + 1 #This is a comment.
=> 2
```

```
irb(main):003:0>
```

As you can see, the line after the hash sign was just ignored and Ruby just evaluated the expression 1 + 1.

In case you are going to start programming using Ruby's programming mode, there will be times that you will want to create multiple lines of comments. You can still use hash signs to create multiple lines. For example:

```
#This is a comment.
#This is another comment.
#This is the last comment.
```

If you do not want to use that method, you can do this by using the =begin and =end keyword. Below is an example on how to use them:

```
=begin
This is a comment
This is another comment.
This is the last comment.
=end
```

All lines after the =begin and before the =end keyword will be treated as comment lines.

Those are just the primary rules in Ruby's syntax. Some commands have syntax of their own. They will be discussed together with the commands themselves.

Chapter 3: Parts of a Statement

You have been seeing the term statement in the previous chapters. As mentioned before, a statement is a combination of keywords, operators, variables, constants, values, expressions, methods, and properties which is translated as a command.

In this chapter, you will know what six of those parts are: variables, constants, keywords, values, operators, and expressions. Let's start with variables.

Variables

In Math, you know that variables are placeholders for values. For example:

x = 1 + 1

x = 2

y = 3

In the previous line, variable x has a value of 2 and variable y has a value of 3. Variables in Ruby (or other programming languages) act the same way – as placeholders. However, unlike in Math, variables in Ruby do not act as placeholders for numbers alone. It can contain different types of values like strings and objects.

To create variables in Ruby, all you need is to assign a value to one. For example:

```
irb(main):001:0> a = 12
```

That example commands Ruby to create a variable named a and assign the number 12 as its value. To check the value of a variable in Ruby's interpreter mode, input a on a new line and press the Enter key. It will produce the result:

```
=> 12
```

A while ago, instead of getting a reply like that from Ruby, you have got this instead:

```
NameError: undefined local variable or method 'a' for main:Object
        from (irb):1
        from C:/Ruby21/bin/irb:11:in '<main>'
```

Technically, the error means that Ruby was not able to find a variable or method with the name a. Now, when you input a, it does not produce that error anymore since you have already created a variable named a.

By the name, in computer programming, the names you give to variables and other entities in the program are called identifiers. Some call them IDs or tokens instead.

There are some set of rules when giving an identifier to a variable. Identifiers can contain letters, numbers, and underscores. A variable identifier must start with a lower case letter or an underscore. It may also contain one or more characters. Also, variable identifiers should not be the same with a keyword or reserved words.

Just like any programming languages, reserved or special keywords cannot be used as identifiers.

Constants

Constants are like variables, but you can only assign a value to them once in your program and their identifiers must start with an uppercase letter. Reassigning a value to them will generate an error or a warning.

Keywords

Keywords are special reserved words in Ruby that perform specific functions and commands. Some of them are placeholder for special values such as true, false, and nil.

The nil value means that the entity that contains it does not have a value. To put it simply, all variables will have the nil value if no value was assigned to it. When they are used and they have nil as their value, Ruby will return a warning if the – w is on.

Values

In Ruby, there are multiple types of values that you can assign in a variable. In programming, they are called literals. In coding Ruby, you will be dealing with these literals every time.

Integers

You can write integers in four forms or numeral systems: decimal, hexadecimal, octal, and binary. To make Ruby understand that you are declaring integers in hexadecimal (base 16), octal (base 8), or binary (base 2), you should use prefixes or leading signs.

If you are going to use octal, use 0 (zero). If you are going to use hexadecimal, use 0x (zero-x). If you are going to use binary, use 0b (zero-b). If you are going to use decimal, there is no need for any optional leading signs.

Depending on the size of the integer, it can be categorized in the class Fixnum or Bignum.

Floating Numbers

Any integer with decimals is considered a floating number. All floating numbers are under the class Float.

Strings

Strings are values inside single or double quotation marks. They are treated as text in Ruby. You can place expression evaluation inside strings without terminating your quotes. You can just insert expressions by using the hash sign and enclosing the expression using curly braces. For example:

```
irb(main):001:0> a = "the sum of 3 and 1 is: #{3 + 1}."
=> "the sum of 3 and 1 is: 4."
```

You can also access variables or constants in Ruby and include them in a string by placing a hash sign (#) before the variable or constant's name. For example:

```
irb(main):001:0> b = "string inside variable."
=> "string inside variable."
irb(main):002:0> b = "You can access a #{b}"
=> "You can access a string inside variable."
```

Arrays

An array is a data type that can contain multiple data or values. Creating arrays in Ruby is simple. Type Array and then follow it with values enclosed inside square brackets. Make sure that you separate each value with a comma. Any exceeding commas will be ignored and will not generate error. For example:

```
irb(main):001:0> arraysample = Array[1, 2, 3]
=> [1, 2, 3]
```

To access a value of an array, you must use its index. The index of an array value depends on its location in the array. For example, the value 2 in the arraysample variable has an index number of 0. The value 2, has an index of 1. And the value 3, has an index of 2. The index increments by 1 and starts with zero.

Below is an example on how to access a value in an array:

```
irb(main):001:0> arraysample[2]
=> 3
```

Hashes or Associative Arrays:

Hashes are arrays that contain paired keys (named index) and values. Instead of a numbered index, you can assign and use keys to access your array values.

```
irb(main):001:0> hashsample = Hash["First" => 1, "Second" = > 2]
=> {"First"=>1, "Second"=>2}
```

To access a hash value, you just need to call it using its key instead of an index number. For example:

```
irb(main):001:0> hashsample["Second"]
=> 2
```

Expressions

Expressions are combinations of operators, variables, values, and/or keywords. Expressions result into a value or can be evaluated by Ruby. A good example of an expression is 1 + 1. In that, Ruby can evaluate that expression and it will result to 2. The plus sign (+) is one of many operators in Ruby.

You can assign expression to a variable. The result of the expression will be stored on the variable instead of the expression itself. For example:

```
irb(main):001:0> a = 1 + 1
=> 2
```

If you check the value of a by inputting a into the shell, it will return 2 not 1 + 1.

As mentioned a while ago, expressions can also contain variables. If you assign a simple or complex expression with a variable to another variable, Ruby will handle all the evaluation. For example:

```
irb(main):001:0> a = 2
=> 2
irb(main):002:0> b = 4
=> 4
irb(main):003:0> c = a + b + 6
=> 12
```

Operators

Operators are symbols or keywords that command the computer to perform operations or evaluations. Ruby's operators are not limited to performing arithmetic operations alone. The following are the operators you can use in Ruby:

Arithmetic Operators

Arithmetic operators allow Ruby to evaluate simple Math expressions. They are: + for addition, - for subtraction, * for multiplication, / for division, % for modulus, and ** for exponent.

Division in Ruby works differently. If you are dividing integers, you will get an integer quotient. If the quotient should have a fractional component or decimal on it, they will be removed. For example:

```
irb(main):001:0> 5 / 2
=> 2
```

If you want to get an accurate quotient with a fractional component, you must perform division with fractional components For example:

```
irb(main):001:0> 5.0 / 2
=> 2.5
```

For those who are unfamiliar with modulus: modulus performs regular division and returns the remainder instead of the quotient. For example:

```
irb(main):001:0> 5 % 2
=> 1
```

Comparison Operators

Ruby can compare numbers, too, with the help of comparison operators. Comparison operations provide two results only: true or false. For example:

```
irb(main):001:0> 1 > 2
=> false
```

The value 1 is less than 2, but not greater than; therefore, Ruby evaluated that the expression is false.

Other comparison operators that you can use in Ruby are: == for has equal value, != for does not have equal value, > for greater than, < for less than, >= for greater than or equal, and <= for less than or equal. There four other comparison operators (===, <=>, .eql?, and .equal?) in Ruby, but you do not need them for now.

Assignment Operators

Assignment operators are used to assign value to operators, properties, and other entities in Ruby. You have already encountered the most used assignment operator, which is the equal sign (=). There are other assignment operators other than that, which are simple combination of the assignment operator (=) and arithmetic operators.

They are += for add and assign, -= for subtract and assign, *= for multiply and assign, /= for divide and assign, % for modulus and assign, and ** for raise and assign.

All of them perform the arithmetic operation and the values they use are the value of the entity on their left and the expression on their right first before assigning the result of the operation to the entity on its left. It might seem confusing, so here is an example:

```
irb(main):001:0> a = 1
=> 1
irb(main):002:0> a += 2
=> 3
```

In the example, variable a was given a value of 1. On the next statement, the add and assign operator was used. After the operation, a's value became 3 because a + 2 = 3. That can also be achieved by doing this:

```
irb(main):001:0> a = 1
=> 1
irb(main):002:0> a = a + 2
=> 3
```

If the value to the right of these operators is an expression that contain multiple values and operators, it will be evaluated first before the assignment operators perform their operations. For example:

```
irb(main):001:0> a = 1
=> 1
irb(main):002:0> a += 3 * 2
=> 7
```

The expression 3 * 2 was evaluated first, which resulted to 6. Then six was added to variable a that had a value of 1, which resulted to 7. And that value value was assigned to variable a.

Other Operators

As you advance your Ruby programming skills, you will encounter more operators. And they are:

Logical Operator: and, or, &&, ||, !, not
Defined Operator: defined?
Reference Operators: ., ::

Chapter 4: Object Oriented Programming

In the previous chapters, you have learned the basics of Ruby programming. Those chapters also serve as your introduction to computer programming since most programming languages follow the same concepts and have similar entities in them. In this chapter, you will learn why some programmers love Ruby.

Ruby is an Object Oriented Programming (OOP) language. Object oriented programming makes use of objects and classes. Those objects and classes can be reused which in turn makes it easier to code programs that require multiple instances of values that are related to each other.

Programming methods can be categorized into two: Procedural and Object Oriented. If you have experienced basic programming before, you mostly have experienced procedural instead of object oriented.

In procedural, your program's code revolves around actions. For example, you have a program that prints what a user will input. It is probable that your program's structure will be as simple as take user input, assign the input to a variable, and then print the content of the variable. As you can see, procedural is a straightforward forward method.

Classes and Objects

Classes are like templates for objects. For example, a Fender Telecaster and a Gibson Les Paul are objects and they are under the electric guitar class.

In programming, you can call those guitars as instances of the class of objects named electric guitars. Each object has its own properties or characteristics.

Objects under the same class have same properties, but the value of those properties may differ or be the same per object. For example, think that an electric guitar's properties are: brand, number of strings, and number of guitar pickups.

Aside from that, each object has its own functions or things that it can do. When it comes to guitars, you can strum all the strings or you can just pick on one string.

If you convert that to Ruby code, that will appear as:

```
class ElectricGuitar
	def initialize
		@brand = “Local”
		@strings = 6
		@pickups = 3
	end
	def strum
```

```
        #Insert statements to execute when strum is called
    end
    def pick
        #Insert statements to execute when strum is called
end
```

Creating a Class

To create a class, you need to use the class keyword and an identifier. Class identifiers have the same syntax rules for constant identifiers. To end the creation of the class, you need to use the end keyword. For example:

```
irb(main):001:0> class Guitar
irb(main):002:1> end
=> nil
```

Creating an Object

Now, you have a class. It is time for you to create an object. To create one, all you need is to think of an identifier and assign the class name and the keyword new to it for it to become an object under a class. For example:

```
irb(main):001:0> fender = Guitar. new
=> #<Guitar:0x1234567>
```

Note: Do not forget to add a dot operator after the class name.

Unfortunately, the class Guitar does not contain anything in it. That object is still useless and cannot be used for anything. To make it useful, you need to add some methods and properties to it.

Methods

This is where it gets interesting. Methods allow your objects to have 'commands' of some sort. In case you want to have multiple lines of statements to be done, placing them under a class method is the best way to do that. To give your classes or objects methods, you will need to use the def (define) keyword. Below is an example:

```
irb(main):001:0> class Guitar
irb(main):002:1> def strum
irb(main):003:2> puts "Starts strumming."
irb(main):004:2> puts "Strumming."
irb(main):005:2> puts "Ends strumming."
irb(main):006:2> end
irb(main):007:1> end
=> :strum
```

Now, create a new object under that class.

```
irb(main):008:0> gibson = Guitar. new
=> #<Guitar:0x1234567>
```

To use the method you have created, all you need is to invoke it using the object. For example:

```
irb(main):009:0> gibson.strum
Starts strumming.
Strumming.
Ends strumming.
=> nil
```

By using the dot operator, you were able to invoke the method inside the gibson object under the Guitar class. All the objects that will be under Guitar class will be able to use that method.

Conclusion

Thank you again for purchasing this book!

I hope this book was able to help you understand how coding in Ruby works.

The next step is to:

- Learn more about flow control tools in Ruby
- Study about the other operators discussed in this book
- Research on how variables inside classes and objects work

Finally, if you enjoyed this book, please take the time to share your thoughts and post a review on Amazon. We do our best to reach out to readers and provide the best value we can. Your positive review will help us achieve that. It'd be greatly appreciated!

Thank you and good luck!

Check Out My Other Books

Below you'll find some of my other popular books that are popular on Amazon and Kindle as well. Simply click on the links below to check them out. Alternatively, you can visit my author page on Amazon to see other work done by me.

C Programming Success in a Day

Python Programming Success in a Day

PHP Programming Professional Made Easy

HTML Professional Programming Made Easy

CSS Programming Professional Made Easy

Windows 8 Tips for Beginners

C Programming Professional Made Easy

JavaScript Programming Made Easy

Rails Programming Professional Made Easy

C ++ Programming Success in a Day

If the links do not work, for whatever reason, you can simply search for these titles on the Amazon website to find them.

www.ingramcontent.com/pod-product-compliance
Lightning Source LLC
Chambersburg PA
CBHW070903070326
40690CB00009B/1978
* 9 7 8 1 5 1 1 4 8 9 0 2 7 *